LEVELLING UP MY ARSE

TheBinMan

Balboa Press books may be ordered through booksellers or by contacting:

Balboa Press
A Division of Hay House
1663 Liberty Drive
Bloomington, IN 47403
www.balboapress.co.uk
UK TFN: 0800 0148647 (Toll Free inside the UK)
UK Local: 02036 956325 (+44 20 3695 6325 from outside the UK)

ISBN: 978-1-9822-8590-6 (sc)
ISBN: 978-1-9822-8591-3 (e)

Print information available on the last page.

Balboa Press rev. date: 05/26/2022

Contents

2066

Levelling up my arse

Self-image is extremely important in leadership wanting to lead people to a bar to celebrate actually requires a reason to celebrate other than your need to indulge your bloated liver and your ravenous ego, wanting to make a speech is about having something to say. The pied piper tune needs to be catchy and entrancing not the arse belches of a bloated little boy intent on indulging the nerve endings between his legs. Leading a nation requires a plan carved from a vision of what is hidden inside a rock. A statue of an athlete in his prime not the musings of a small child playing with clay and begging for praise for his miniscule creations.

Bullying has more than one victim as it permeates the soul of the bully when he unexpectedly realises it is his own inferiority that has made him even smaller than his victims. There is a nobility to suffering that creates legends. It is this legendary status that the bully seeks which he ironically creates in his victims.

Protesting and or revolution will never defeat the entitled classes as these acts invite suppression backed by a strong sense of media self-righteousness which manifests in negative results (like the miners strike in the 1980's) which always result in the strong feelings of the masses fading and the initial energies of warring classes that commence revolution are dependent upon group continued mass synchronisation and frankly the energies cannot be sustained in working class groups beyond the millennia of entitled classes motivation to protect themselves and their possessions from the masses. The entitled classes fear of being toppled is significantly more sustainable group motivator than any temporary indignation of the masses which is often fleeting and disingenuous as it never has the media on its side and the masses by definition are waiting to be led and have been systematically trained to follow the rules set by the entitled classes. Therefore, the only way that the masses can succeed is by playing the games invented by the capitalists' and utilise the rules of the entitled classes and then beating them at their own game. This strategy is more sustainable as humans are naturally greedy and self-centred and competitive which is how the world has got in this mess in the first place. The beauty of this strategy is you cannot be prosecuted for being an ambitious capitalist and its almost impossible to put a white-collar criminal behind bars. Last but not least we can afford to take the risks as we have nothing to lose.

Preface & Introduction

Levelling up is a political term coined by the British conservative political group whom decided in about 2018 that if they were to stay in power in England, now that they had lost Scotland and Wales and Northern Ireland, through consistently being selfish to their own needs and as a by product letting people not in Westminster down or double crossing them completely to suit the needs of Londoners and rich people in general. There reasoning therefore is that if they are to stay in power, they need to promise to help northern people in England to realise their dreams at least for the children of the Northerners who are likely to vote. This promise is wrapped in the Brexit referendum as that was when northerners switched from Labour to conservative in droves and the so-called red wall in the North became multicoloured and interspersed with the conservative blue and liberal yellow. So, to stay in power it is English voters that matter and there aren't enough southern seats to keep them in power. The main flaw with this strategy, is that they have no intention to keep this promise and will soon be found wanting in the north. At time of writing, they have already reduced the railway spending in the North due to being heavily over budget. Not those budgets are ever kept in the south. The most astounding fact about levelling up is it cannot happen due to the fact that we live in a small nation of class warfare. There are only so many university places in oxford and Cambridge and the higher classes will not sacrifice those places for people whose IQ is actually determined by the occupations of their parents, and almost entirely by the wealth of those parents. This is the same for the Hospitals and the banks and the insurance companies and the police and the army. In fact, children of rich parents are immensely privileged and have no self-perception as they assume that this privilege is as a direct result of their own efforts and natural selection visa vie their gene pool being of a higher intellectual status. Quite frankly they are brought up to believe that northerners are poor because they are stupid and ape like and are naturally lazy and don't want to work. When in actual fact the opposite is true. Northerners know they have to work extremely hard to survive and to overcome southern prejudices. Worse still, interbreeding in the south has developed a long line of chinless wonders and thick but decent university types, whom achieve very little in their longer lives other than social graces. A very over rated quality in the English persona. The real engine room of the British Isles lies far away from London Cambridge and Oxford. The trouble is it is subservient to the Southern elite because all of the northern and Scottish and Welsh elite follow the money south without a thought for their childhood peer group. Once among the London elite I'm afraid they behave in a similarly dismissive fashion to those in the lower classes. This of course is human nature. However, it has been the case in England for over 1000 years, since William the conqueror set up home in London to remain closer to his true home in northern France. His desires for the north to succeed centred on gifting land to his friends as rewards for favours and deeds done to support his reign as tax collector to support his ambitions for more land in France.

With the exception of wars in the north related to Scotland Wales and Ireland, fought to install back door locks to England's lands, this disdain for the North and the poor has continued and become more acute as London has become a world trade centre in modern times. People will cite the English civil war as being fought all over the North, but what were they fighting over? Power in the South. Who rules parliament or the crown? Parliament then was only the Lords, poor people had no vote, but had to fight nevertheless. Also, from history we have the northern war known as the war of the roses between Lancashire and Yorkshire. What was it about? Who will be king? Which is the real line of succession? Nothing to do with the Northern people at all, other than the fact they had to enlist and fight again to decide it. So, in one sweeping historical simplification I suggest that since William the Conqueror saw the north as full of Serfs to work and to tax to fuel his wars Northerners are still seen by the South as serfs to work and tax, with no desires or dreams of our own. Therefore, I have titled this book 2066, in respect for the 1000th anniversary of the battle of Hastings when Northerners in England lost their humanity.

It is my dearest hope that within the next 44 years, as it is 2022 as I write, the North and whosoever decides to join her will have become independent of London and the crown. This being the only possible way to level up this split nation. We must rise up economically to become equal as there is no chance whatsoever that the south will lift us up to their coveted status and luxury, because by definition they will no longer have privilege, only equality. Equality is a desire of the poor but it is the pied piper of the rich and powerful. It makes a pleasant tune until you realise your children died in another man's war. This race for material wealth, long life with health and education, may seem a shallow goal to the more enlightened amongst us but please do not let these high-minded thoughts cloud your decision making. Life is a struggle and it's the biggest game that any of us will ever play. It's a three-dimensional game of chess where all the pieces have free will and the prizes are power and influence, on a global scale. The good news is you will get on average 90 years of play so please adopt a long-term strategy and execute it ruthlessly as nobody will stand in your way as long as you're not seen to be breaking the law. So go for it, big time, don't hold back, don't be talked down from your main goal which is to ensure all of your descendants have a better life than you. Remember white collar crime is hardly suffering, so as long as you avoid violence you can get away with murder, get a short sentence in a holiday camp prison and early parole for a fake illness if you can half way act?

So, if you're with me lets rise up to their lofty material inherited lifestyle which will take time, organisation, patience and money and we will need allies, but we have huge advantages, we have examples from history and the internet to assist us achieve our rightful place amongst the fully employed and fairly paid. Its time to start working to rectify this thousand-year class war and today is the first day of the rest of our lives. Hopefully by 2066 we will have more free time with the advent of robotics which we must embrace and not protest about like we did the spinning jenny. Robots will be our liberators not our oppressors. Just ensure you use your free time wisely to make plans and money.

Having been born in the lower classes to a poor family I have become independently wealthy and I will give you my thoughts on how the levelling up can begin. I hope it is helpful and entertaining as a grand plan to lift ourselves up by our bootstraps and most of all I hope it gains a massive following amongst the poorest class in this country the northern working class.

Education

In every aspect of life, we must significantly raise our standards and this must begin with education. We must raise our children to believe they are in charge of their destiny and that each and everyone of them can be a billionaire within their lifetime, it is not difficult to do, look at the Americans and the Chinese, self-belief in themselves and their country are sewn into their brains from birth. We as parents must not continue training children to be humble and accepting of our status as our children's status will be far superior to our own, which given our humility and embarrassing need to apologise for our existence will not be difficult. There is no reason that teachers at private schools are worth the extra money they get paid other than rich peoples need to assert their dominance in society and have the most successful children so they pay more to attract the best teachers to their schools. Many of those teachers are from poorer northern communities. The mistake that these old-fashioned schools make is that they convince the kids to aim high to be captains of industry or prime ministers or generals, all noble professions but those ambitions do not suit the modern world. The modern world is all about money and making as much as you can as quickly as you can, this is the new mantra of all classes as only money satisfies, look how unhappy Boris Johnson is having followed his teachers' instructions to the letter but finds himself earning less than he would feel he deserves and therefore finding alternative ways to supplement his income. So, its obvious, our school mantra will be to become self employed and learn the skills of an entrepreneur. This will certainly improve our class wealth distribution and will create millions of jobs over the next 44 years in places where jobs are needed. This will significantly improve productivity as self employed people work harder and longer than employees as they know their earnings are directly related to their own work ethic unlike employees whom just do the bare minimum so as not to get sacked. This single most important doctrine will enable us to not only compete but to win alongside southerners.

So, we need to quickly decide which are our best schools and headmasters and pay them based on delivering success in a wide variety of skill sets. Attracting teachers into poorer areas should be easy to begin as house price differentials will be attractive for relocating. As the schools achieve better results than southern public schools house prices in the poorer areas will rise significantly making everybody richer as house buying is massively influenced by the school performance tables.

We need to repeat the above process for colleges and universities in time for the first year of school leavers to join the perfect colleges and universities, sponsored by local employers whom get the pick of the best graduates thereby giving free education to our young adults, whom remain loyal to each employer for 3 to 5 years minimum. We will need teams of experts ranking employers and students for suitability to the scheme and each other, drawing up contracts between both parties which are legally binding. We need not exclude southern or rich kids from these institutions, in fact we need to encourage migration of rich kids into our areas until they have inherited their parent's money, thereby migrating funds to poorer regions by stealth. Plus, competition is the building block of excellence so the more the merrier. Within a generation we will have our own Eton, Cambridge and Oxford and we will be able to retain our most gifted people and maybe have attracted some of their most gifted children into our fairer self-employed anti discriminatory society. Why discriminate if it doesn't turn a profit? Put another way the more customers the merrier, inclusion is an entrepreneur's lifeblood. Who would he/she not sell to?

Employment

We must begin attracting as many investments into our communities. This means forgetting our trade union upbringing and abandoning our socialist consciences. Yes, this will be our greatest sacrifice after generations of our families fought so hard to achieve the rights that the world now enjoys, like shorter working hours, holiday pay and health care. Those battles and wars are over its as good as its going to get. Its time we competed for the best employers and we helped them maximise profits, otherwise they will invest elsewhere, and quite frankly already are. We must decide between being the highest unemployed regions with the highest morals or the fully employed and richest with compromised morals, and we must teach our children how to become self-employed, competitive and highly sought-after mercenaries the world has ever seen. We must say yes more often to all investors and we must tax employers as little as possible or forever watch Irelands youths take our place in world economics. It has taken over 100 years for Sinn Fein to become the masters of Northern Ireland which will lead to a united free Ireland within a couple of decades. So, you see what a long-term strategy can achieve if you dedicate your lives and your children's lives to a just cause and you stay focussed no matter the adversity placed in front of you. Pain and misery are fleeting memories in the light of raw and joyful success and the longer and more painful the process the greater the rejoicing will be.

We must be willing to deal with anyone who is willing to build and employ in our communities and we must welcome them with open arms and host them like kings and queens of old. We need to be known around the world as the home of innovation and industry at any cost. We must reward our employers by buying their products and buying their shares as our own investments. We need to remind our children which employers put food on their tables and educated them and paid their mortgages. We must create competition from employers to seek our land and our people's willingness to work for them in a compliant and sub servient manner. Let the rest of the country seek improvement of employment rights and union membership you will not lose out as all ships rise at high tide regarding rights, especially those that carried on serving loyally., more importantly the message gets out that your loyalty to your employers is paramount and profitable. I know I cannot believe I am writing these words and hoping for them to come true after a lifetime of voting Labour, but unfortunately what I strongly advocate is the only way to win what we seek for our children. Equality by constant competition. We must lead by example and we must start immediately as the clock is ticking. Let's be the generation that made a sea change and a difference. Which brings us neatly to a hot topic, The Environment.

The Environment

This project can only be led by the consumer. Capitalism has a way of influencing people to vote with their wallet. Products and or organisations that are bad for the planet will naturally die out. No need to accelerate the process out of a sense of panic. Darwin's theory of natural selection works even better within the confines of capitalism. The lifeblood of capitalism is capital and unless your business plan or corporate strategy is centred around saving the plant or the whales or the gorillas you will not receive capital or sales. Your organisation will die. Not least because nobody will want to work for you. Look at Abercrombie & Fitch a deeply racist and elitist belief system which was quickly uncovered and protested against and died swiftly as a result. There are examples of industries that were so rich that they flew in the face of common decency like the Tobacco industry in the 50's and 60's but which eventually change or die. Sure, the planet is dying but please put this into context its impossible to wreck a planet that has existed so long and morphed into what it is today. The real concern of the environmentalists is that humans will become extinct, and of course they will, because they are a virus and deserve to die. But that should not distract you from the immediacy of having unemployed children and drug fuelled porn hungry grandchildren laying ahead in your lifetime. Get a grip, take their future into your life plan. Do something for your unborn descendants. Start today. Make money for them to inherit, so they can buy robots that don't shit or piss or eat or drink because they will be a refreshing change for the planet compared to us humans. As we were a refreshing change to the dinosaurs.

Banking and Cash system

We must resist all attempts to remove cash and bitcoins. These are the currencies of the tax dodging knights of the capitalist's system. We need them as they are our competitive advantage over the flawed lives of the privileged southerners whom are trapped in their moral purgatory lie which permeates and perpetuates their inter-generational law-abiding church going hypocrisy.

Being openly gay I imagine is a wonderful experience and a massive power shift takes place, I believe when a gay person outs themselves as they are no longer vulnerable. Being openly capitalist and bling I imagine is an empowering existence. You are hated but untouchable. Your reputation says yes you can feel superior to me but who has all the happiness and fun? ME ME ME ME ME ME ME!

Don't fall into the mind trap of having pretentions about your status, or worse trying to enclose your mind in the casings of other people's mind traps. Your worth is known by you do not subject yourself to other people's valuations. Celebrate your money and your possession's if nothing else for the increased value put on them by the green-eyed monsters.

Enjoyment

The ruling classes have two weaknesses, they cannot be seen to lose face or be dishonourable as they are taught in church schools and at home about shame and honour, consequently their money must not be mentioned as money should not be their motivation. They cannot use it to satisfy their human instincts to be top dog, therefore we can destroy them with phycological warfare. The more we are proud of our money and our material objects the more they can be disgusted and exponentially jealous and over time the tide will turn in favour of a bling lifestyle which will cause them to join in our game and start to spend and that's when we take it off them. Let's face it their millennia of austerity and thriftiness has not educated them on haggling or dealing with clever salesmen. They cannot even banter as its not taught in their universities. Once we have them enjoying themselves, they are like low hanging fruit. There will be a massive wealth transfer. Trust funds will be emptied in one generation. This has started with the internet and the phenomenon called home traders and bitcoin millionaires. More of the same please younger generation.

Housing

The 2008/2009 financial crash which resulted in a huge increase in the price of assets, created an additional huge increase in buy to let schemes evolving into a monumental issue for baby boomers whom cannot take it with them when they die. A fact that they have convinced themselves is not inevitable. Here's the problem. What happened when most of the landed gentry had to sell their stately homes to pay the inheritance tax bill? Well, we have that situation again. Vast numbers of houses will be released onto the market over the next 30 years resulting in the lowering of house prices and bargains for those people resident in those houses currently paying ridiculous rental prices in areas where all of the best schools are. The baby boomers are quite happy taking these rentals as a pension supplement and are busy living like kings and queens at the renter's expense. However, this corrupt tryst between baby boomers and the banks has resulted in record equity in housing stocks and the government has record national debts and has started taxing these property companies to the extent that the baby boomers dare not sell the assets to be taxed massively on the profits. This has created an additional huge increase in buy to let schemes evolving into a monumental issue for baby boomers whom cannot take it with them when they die. A fact that they have convinced themselves is not inevitable. So, the people that can afford them and are most desirous to buy them already live in them. The banks or other mortgagees will be only too happy to lend the residents the money to buy them otherwise they run the risk of letting their assets overly depreciate. This will only take ten years to flush through the system and the houses will return to their pre funeral prices and a huge transfer of wealth will have taken place. Hopefully the next generation of buy to let owners will buy commercial property which is supported by the tax man as 60% of tax collected locally is in commercial property rates so future governments will increase tax incentives to the self-employed, which are already generous for those of you who own a SSIPP or a SSAS as they need shops to continue otherwise domestic rates will need to triple for local councils to continue in existence. Remember the poll tax riots?

Shopping

On Line shopping is cheaper than real estate shopping, because it avoids tax costs, employment costs and property costs. The three corner stones of human financial existence. How do we run a country without tax? Worse how de we defend it internally or externally? If less than 50% of the population has a job that is generous enough to cause the worker to pay tax? How do people pay bills, drive cars, socialise, watch television, or pay mortgages or house rents or council tax or utility bills or VAT?

Do we all live on universal credit? And who will give us that Universal credit? Nobody volunteers tax anymore! Ask the chancellor.

We must urgently change our habits or we will make ourselves redundant. We must shop locally and support our local facilities, despite the extra costs, or there will be no work for our children. On line shopping is the enemy of the people and will kill employment before robots get here in numbers. We are being led to the edge of the cliff like lemmings. The extra money you pay for each item underpins the financial world as we know it. I'm sure you would not trust any political party to reinvent our financial system once it disappears. The committee that does that will design a camel not a horse. We will get to our destination but we will be very uncomfortable and our clothes will stink, and it will only work in extreme conditions. Not to mention the spitting and the biting en route.

Sports

If bad choices like smoking driving and drinking invite higher taxes then good choices should be rewarded. This is already prevalent in gentlemen's clubs and golf clubs in the UK.

To control the obesity and general health crisis all sport must be tax free to encourage participation and support. Maybe all clubs could redevelop as registered charities that are non-profitable which has the added advantage of stopping greedy billionaires taking ownership to wash cash through and into their enterprises. This would also create a more level playing field and ensure supporter power and reset player wages and attitudes to humane as opposed to obscene levels.

Travel

Business travel is essential if you are to establish a relationship with your customers and your suppliers. Physically meeting someone gives so many more opportunities to build a relationship and it is also far more rewarding for all concerned. I'm saying do mix business with pleasure. The world is built on nepotism. Which means it's a natural human instinct to look after people close to you. So, make your business relationships your friends and family, especially powerful or influential people. Make them your family. I know its shallow but trust me it works. People not involved will see through it and hate you for it. So that's even more reason to do it. It shows your working in the right direction, and the complainers are not and are jealous of your success. Now you know who are your enemies. It's so simple.

Holiday travel should be in support of all of your allies, not your enemies. It's a time when you do the opposite to austerity so spend wisely and look after your own, and they will reciprocate in appreciation, and the nepotism becomes exponential.

Transport

When travelling try to take the modes of transport that are longest in duration and try to meet as many people as you can. When travelling with friends and family do the same and get to know them better and sell them something that enhances your business. It may be just an idea but influence them to your advantage. They will see through it but will not complain because like you they are just trying to kill the boredom of the journey. Tip everyone that serves you it will increase your self esteem enormously and your sense of self-importance, and money makes the world go around.

Congratulations you have effectively made your travel and Subsistence tax deductible.

Socialising

All of your social websites are to be used to promote your products and services and those of your customers and your suppliers. Work hard to make everyone around you rich and they will reciprocate. Its how the rich and famous have been bleeding you dry for centuries. Get in on the act unashamedly.

Business

Look after your customers suppliers and staff but negotiate hard as they always want less than they ask for and certainly have a hidden agenda. Get to know each person's strengths and weaknesses and use this knowledge to your advantage but ensure it's a win win conclusion, as life is long and you need allies not enemies. The soul

Our Soul is our self-worth

The meaning of life is a constantly developing subjective measurement of self-worth.

Our soul is our mind and it is measured daily by its self-worth and we all have power over each other and ourselves, and if we abuse that power, we chip away at the vessel of self-worth which is our sanity. Good deeds improve our self-worth and even small bad deeds chip away at our self-worth. Everybody's soul is different but our need for sanity is the same and it is that which stops us disrespecting each other. disrespecting each other is insanity as it disrespects our own worth and therefore our own souls. Losing your self-worth is to lose your soul which is an act of mental suicide.

Every human entity has a soul, newspapers, businesses, logos, icons, households, teams, countries, religions, as they are all the subject of the human mind. Which is why they all are capable of mutual or self-destruction. Our self-worth is constantly changing and developing as we test our souls against each other and ourselves. The most tested sane souls are the wisest souls and should be respected the most. Life is a revelation of our souls and is the main reason that we strive to test our minds and improve or destroy our self-worth. It is therefore the reason for our existence and propagation. It is also the reason why so many of us believe our souls live forever as it seems insanity for these revelations to be deleted by death. However, in reality it is the act of sudden deletion at any moment that inspires us to live life to the fullest and become the wisest soul that we can. This leads me to the conclusion that Buddha or Mohammed is God as he has the necessary credentials to be our greatest earthly soul and therefore our greatest example by which to measure our soul.

Competition

Know their strengths and weaknesses and use it to undercut them and ruin their confidence at every opportunity. They are definitely doing the same to you as the business environment is cut throat and dog eat dog. The more subtly you can do this the more influential you will become.

Prejudice

In sales and purchasing hold no prejudices at all every sale is a bonus and will lead to more sales. Business is in fact the most anti racist mode of living. Stupid people stay poor due to their prejudices as this choice limits your growth in business.

Bullying

Bullying is the most soul destroying and joyless method of gaining power as its only a matter of time before you realise how weak and insecure it makes you look, and how it eats away at your soul. Exude confidence and assist everyone to achieve peace and tranquillity whilst promoting your products and services so that they are associating your products and services with peace and tranquillity.

Inheritance

Look at the next generation as your future sales and marketing team. Ensure they are able to carry your torch for generations to come. Help them to enjoy the benefits of their inheritance whilst you live as it is part of their education.

Health

Your mental health and general longevity are paramount to your success. You must outlive your enemies and support your allies for as long as you possibly can. You must survive and provide that is your role. Its boring at times but amuse yourself by hatching a bigger and more outrageous marketing strategy. Every thought and dream you have is precious and you must pursue it until it worn out and then you must drop it like a hot potato and choose your next best recent thought as this is your life's fresh passion.

Tax

Avoid it this is for the mugs, don't break the law but exploit every tax dodge you can and try inventing new ones all the time. Everyone else is especially the law makers and the law keepers. They use their privilege to line their pockets and those of their friends and relatives.

Opportunity

Everything is an opportunity especially bad news. You just need to find a way to use your inside knowledge on each development in your life to see the upside for your business. A good trick is to reverse the situation to let the money flow. The end of petroleum will mean lots of petrol stations will be dirt cheap etc etc.

Politics

Look for alliances and marry up with the party that is closest to your causes. Who can give your business grants? Which party is seeking more autonomy for the regions?

Why reinvent the wheel? These parties have hundreds of clever people over hundreds of years, take a piggy back from the most suitable. They will be happy to increase their numbers.

Royalty. The queen and duke of Edinburgh have served you well, but that's over and let's face it the next lot are self-centred and lacking in self-discipline. Don't waste time here. They will not promote your products without a massive back hander so go for social networking instead. They will not touch you with a barge pole or with more respect than something nasty on their shoe. Don't waste time here.

Lightning Source UK Ltd.
Milton Keynes UK
UKHW050711140622
404397UK00005B/41